Every Mother
Is a
Queen
Mother

Every Mother Is a Queen Mother

And Other Outspoken Observations from The Red Cat Society

Created by Kevin Whitlark • Written by Patrick Regan

Andrews McMeel
Publishing

Kansas City

Every Mother Is a Queen Mother

For information, write Andrews McMeel Publishing,
an Andrews McMeel Universal company,
4520 Main Street, Kansas City, Missouri 64111.

06 07 08 09 10 WKT 10 9 8 7 6 5 4 3 2 1

ISBN-13: 978-0-7407-5739-6

ISBN-10: 0-7407-5739-3

Library of Congress Control Number: 2005932618

Book design by Holly Camerlinck

www.andrewsmcmeel.com

Every Mother
Is a
Queen
Mother

This book is dedicated to Christine Maher Whitlark
and Patricia McCunniff Regan, two amazing women who,
between them, gave birth to twenty-two children,
including the author and the illustrator. As the youngest
of our respective families, we are eternally grateful
that you didn't know when to quit.

—K.W. and P.R.

INTRODUCTION

Motherhood. It's not just a job. It's not just an adventure. It's the willing acceptance that you will never again—for the next twenty years or so at least—enjoy a leisurely meal, pass two consecutive days without doing laundry, or speak uninterrupted on the phone.

We at The Red Cat Society, like our two-legged sisters in spirit—those lovely ladies of The Red Hat Society—believe that the female of the species should be celebrated and revered at all times, regardless of their reproductive track record. But we hold an extraspecial place in our hearts for women who have experienced the slings and arrows, the sacrifices, skinned knees, and simple joys of child rearing and raising.

All mothers deserve the royal treatment, and those who have reached the exalted status of "experienced mother" (which we believe happens around age fifty) are truly queens of their domains.

Mothers-of-a-certain-age, this one's for you.

Mother *noun* **a**: a female parent **b**: a woman in authority **c**: the font of all life **d**: she who must be obeyed.

Queen *noun* **a**: a woman eminent in rank, power, or attractions **b**: a goddess, the supreme ruler of a domain **c**: an attractive woman; *especially*: a beauty contest winner

Researchers at The Red Cat Society have determined that the genius who coined the phrase "working mother" is also responsible for the brilliant redundancies "closed fist," "plan ahead," "advance warning," "foreign imports," and "bare naked."

If evolution really works,
how come mothers only have two hands?

—ED DUSSAULT

HOW TO BE A
Queen Mother:

Refuse to deal with trivialities.

"The kids are hungry? Let them eat cake."

Treat the royal court well.

Never appear at official public functions without your crown.

The first art to be learned by a ruler is to endure envy.
—SENECA

THREE-STEP GUIDE TO THE PROPER Queen Mother WAVE

1. Raise arm, bent approximately 70° at elbow.
2. Hold fingers together, slightly cupped.
3. With arm held stiff, rotate paw slightly from side to side.
4. Smile pleasantly at the commoners.

THE Red Cat SOCIETY'S HANDY ROYAL TITLE CREATOR

(Because every mother is royalty.)

Directions: Mix and match Royal Title + "of" (optional) + Hobby or Personality Trait

Royal Title

Princess
Duchess
High Priestess
Maiden
Lady
Baroness
Countess
Dame

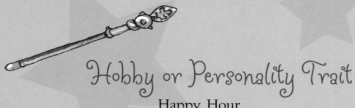

Hobby or Personality Trait

Happy Hour
Garage Sales
Sleeping In
Scrapbooking
Accessorizing
Culinary Creations
Digital Photography
Stuck in the '60s

EXAMPLES:

High Priestess of Happy Hour

Duchess of Digital Photography

Dame Stuck-in-the-'60s

A suburban mother's role is to deliver children obstetrically once, and by car for ever after.

—PETER DE VRIES

I take a very practical view of raising children.
I put a sign in each of their rooms:
CHECKOUT TIME IS 18 YEARS.

—ERMA BOMBECK

Queen Mothers ARE ALWAYS LADIES-IN-WAITING

Waiting for them to be born

Waiting for them to talk

Waiting for them to go to school

Waiting for them to move out

Waiting for them to call

Waiting for them to make you a grandmother

WISDOM FROM
THE Queen Mother CAT

Children should be *seen* (doing chores)
and heard (saying "Please," "Thank you,"
and "Dinner was delicious.").

The most remarkable thing about my mother is that for thirty years she served the family nothing but leftovers.

The original meal has never been found.

—CALVIN TRILLIN

My mother's menu consisted of two choices:
take it or leave it.

—BUDDY HACKETT

MOM'S PLACE

There are three ways to get something done:
Do it yourself, employ someone to do it,
or forbid your children from doing it.

—MONTA CRANE

When love is gone,
there's always justice.
And when justice is gone,
there's always force.
And when force is gone,
there's always Mom.

—LAURIE ANDERSON

A mother is

someone who knows that a family vacation *isn't*.

DIFFERENCES BETWEEN MOTHERS AND FATHERS

A mother takes the kids to the dentist, doctor, and orthodontist. Dad takes kids fishing, camping, and to the movies.

A mother stays up all night with her sick child, soothing fevered heads
and calming upset tummies.
Dad brings them home a new comic book after work.

A mother spends endless hours on the phone counseling her grown
children in times of emotional crisis.
Dad gives them a punch on the arm and writes them a check.

Every successful family needs
one laugh starter, one hand holder,
one peacemaker, and one rule enforcer.
In other words, Mom.

A mother is

someone who knows that a good night's sleep is
what everyone else in the house had.

THE GREAT CYCLE OF MOTHERHOOD

Anticipation

Aggravation

Sleep Deprivation

Frustration

Rejuvenation

Elation

Mortification

A mother is

someone who maintains the impression
that she truly prefers the heel of the bread, the
crust of the pie, the cookies with burned bottoms,
and the chair with the wobbly leg.

A ROYAL DECREE
FROM HER MAJESTY

*An untidy home shall be considered evidence
of a full, well-balanced life.*

THE FOUR STAGES OF MOTHERHOOD

1.

Clueless but Eager
(a very short stage)

2.

Exhausted but Willing
(a very long stage)

3.
Unflappable and Unfoolable

4.
Ready to Do It
All Over Again

PHOTOS

There's a lot more to being a woman than being a mother, but there's a hell of a lot more to being a mother than most people suspect.

—ROSEANNE

I want my children to have
all the things I couldn't afford.
Then I want to move in
with them.

—PHYLLIS DILLER

Mother always said
that honesty was the best policy,
and money isn't everything.
She was wrong about
other things, too.

—GERALD BARZAN

A Mother's Lexicon

Mother-hood:
What you wished you could hide under when your three-year-old threw a tantrum in the middle of the grocery store.

Matricide:

The side of the bed that kids invariably came to when they were feeling "pukey" at three a.m.

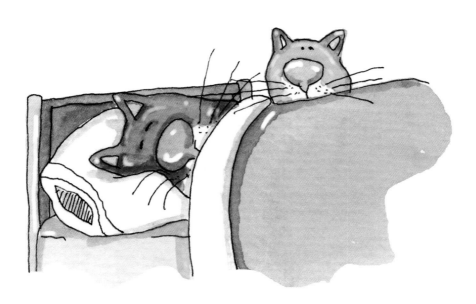

Mometary Policy:
The detailed set of rules that kept the household
from descending into total chaos.

Momentoes:
Those adorable handmade art pieces
(usually including painted macaroni shells)
that you unfailingly received on Mother's Day.

Motherbored:

How you felt watching your third consecutive
Saturday morning soccer game.
(Though you never let them know it.)

Mom-entum:

The only thing that kept you going at the end of the day.

Mother Lode:

The mountain of laundry deposited on your floor when your kid came home on break from college.

Mother Tongue:

What you tried to hold when your only daughter announced
that she had decided to elope . . . to a jungle in Ecuador.

Red Cat Society
Role Model: Cleopatra

Distinctive Traits

Powerful: Last pharaoh of Egypt

Brainy: Spoke nine languages

Womanly wiles: Julius Caesar and Mark Antony each fought wars for her

Beauty secret: Bathed in goat's milk

Other beauty secret: Killed herself at age thirty-nine

Red Cat SOCIETY
ROLE MODEL: BETTE DAVIS

DISTINCTIVE TRAITS

Nickname: The First Lady of Film

Gutsy: Sued Warner Bros. for better roles; got better roles

Unapologetic: Taught three generations of women how to look cool smoking

Persistent: Married four times (three children)

Star-making role: Spoiled, flirtatious Southern belle in *Jezebel*

Quote: "If you have never been hated by your child, you have never been a parent."

Red Cat Society
Role Model:
Rose Fitzgerald Kennedy

Distinctive Traits

Claim to fame: Matriarch of Kennedy clan

Prolific: Mother to nine children, including two U.S. senators and one president

Persistent: Lived to be 105; spunky till the end

Quote: "Any woman who still thinks marriage is a fifty-fifty proposition is only proving that she doesn't understand either men or percentages."

When your mother asks, "Do you want a piece of advice?" it's a mere formality. It doesn't matter if you answer yes or no. You're going to get it anyway.

—ERMA BOMBECK

GIFTS MOTHERS *Really* WANT FROM THEIR GROWN CHILDREN

1. All of your junk out of her basement.
2. Clear, step-by-step instructions on how to program the damn thermostat.
3. An invitation to dinner (at your house if you can cook, at a restaurant if not).
4. For you to be a darling three-year-old again, or, failing that . . .
5. A grandchild!

Young mothers

record meticulous details in baby books.

"Let's see, the first tooth arrived on March 27 at 6:03 p.m."

Experienced mothers

see them as more a work of fiction.

Young mothers

call the Ask-a-Nurse hotline for splinter advice.

Experienced mothers

can cure diphtheria with the right combination of Children's Tylenol, Dimetapp, and Pedialyte.

Young mothers

want to share every minute of their precious child's day.

Experienced mothers

want just one single friggin' minute to themselves.

A Mother's Guide to the Royal Treatment

The time to relax
is when you don't have time for it.

—SIDNEY J. HARRIS

Treat Yourself to the Ultimate Home Spa Experience

cucumber slices

"I may not feel any better, but I taste delicious."

almond-sugar body scrub

rosemary-honey hair conditioner

avocado-lavender hand cream

Keep your nails in good repair.
You never know when you might need them.

MOTHER ARCHETYPES

(Remind you of anyone you know?)

Gilded Glenda

The kids are thriving, the husband's company just went public,
the hair is perfect, and the house is spotless.
Mothering philosophy: Leave it to nanny.

Starstruck Sue

The ultimate stage mother. Always dreamed of
being thanked in an Oscar speech.
Mothering philosophy: Smile, darling! Smile!

Frantic Flo

Late for work, chronic loser of car keys,
occasionally forgets names of own children.
Mothering philosophy: Another day, another crisis.

Earth Mama

Buys organic, drives hybrid, enjoys feeling smugly superior.
Mothering philosophy: Think globally. Parent locally.

Major Mom

Dinner at 1800 hours, bath at 1830, bed at 1900. Reveille at 0700.
Mothering philosophy: No discipline, no dessert.

Rowdy Rhonda

Always ready to roll up the rug and have some fun.
Mothering philosophy: When the mice are away, the cat will play.

QUEEN MOTHER MILESTONES WORTH CELEBRATING

★ Last child successfully potty trained.

★ An entire month with no trip to ER, pediatrician, dentist, or orthodontist.

★ A kid who's old enough to drive to his/her own soccer practice.

★ Fiftieth Birthday
(aka Coronation Day):
The day when a mother truly
becomes a Queen Mother.

★ College Graduation:
The kids are now officially
smart enough to make a living.

The best way to keep children home
is to make the home atmosphere pleasant—
and let the air out of the tires.

—DOROTHY PARKER

$\mathcal{N}$o matter how old
a mother is, she watches her
middle-aged children for
signs of improvement.

—FLORIDA SCOTT-MAXWELL

$\mathcal{I}$ refuse to admit I'm
more than fifty-two,
even if that does
make my sons illegitimate.

—LADY NANCY ASTOR

A "Mature" Mother's
Serenity Prayer

God, grant me the serenity to accept wrinkles, curves, and
graying hair;

The courage to wear a red hat which doesn't suit me;

And the wisdom to realize that all fashion models are
air-brushed anorexics.

Time is a dressmaker specializing in alterations.
—FAITH BALDWIN

THE EMPTY NEST
(HOW IT FEELS)

"The last twenty-five years were a complete blur."

What to Do
When the Last Kitten
Moves Out:
A Mother's Coping Guide

1. Don't panic. Silence is disconcerting but won't hurt you.
2. When the dust clears, try to remember if you are married. If so, reacquaint yourself with your spouse. (He's that guy you occasionally bumped into in the hallway.)
3. Keep busy, but avoid the urge to rashly pick up any hobbies that involve hot glue, silk flowers, or gingham fabric.
4. Call your friends to see which ones have survived raising children. Invite them over to catch up on the last few decades.

A FINAL THOUGHT . . .

Motherhood is like Albania—
you can't trust the
descriptions in the books,
you have to go there.

—MARNI JACKSON